Matthias Heise

Climb Beyond

The future of indoor climbing

Anchor Compact

Heise, Matthias: Climb Beyond: The future of indoor climbing. Hamburg, Anchor Academic Publishing 2014
Original title of the thesis: «buchtitel»

Buch-ISBN: 978-3-95489-199-3
PDF-eBook-ISBN: 978-3-95489-699-8
Druck/Herstellung: Anchor Academic Publishing, Hamburg, 2014

Bibliografische Information der Deutschen Nationalbibliothek:
Die Deutsche Nationalbibliothek verzeichnet diese Publikation in der Deutschen Nationalbibliografie; detaillierte bibliografische Daten sind im Internet über http://dnb.d-nb.de abrufbar

Bibliographical Information of the German National Library:
The German National Library lists this publication in the German National Bibliography. Detailed bibliographic data can be found at: http://dnb.d-nb.de

© Anchor Academic Publishing, ein Imprint der Diplomica® Verlag GmbH
http://www.diplom.de, Hamburg 2014
Printed in Germany

Table of Contents

1. Description of the product

"Climb Beyond" is a summary for full featured service in the indoor climbing market with the goal to make this sport more attractive and enjoyable to everyone. The key product is a device that can observe any climbing route and track a climber on it. This tracking information can be re-projected by a laser beam onto the climbing wall enabling any inexperienced climber to get immediate help while being stuck on the wall. The information can also be used for later analyzing and teaching. Once installed, this product will enable visitors to get a much better climbing experience and advance further more easily.

2. Market need

Indoor climbing is a fun sport for urbanized people with a highly increasing market. Most climbing facilities are located in short distance of people's home and reachable without long traveling. Neither special background knowledge nor special physical condition is needed to just start climbing. It perfectly fits the trend of adrenalin sports where people who are stressed by daily life just want to cross the physical borders of what they are capable of. Climbing forces you to face your fear of height, your fear of falling and your fear of being secured by a thin line that is hold by second person that you have to trust. But it gives you the joy of succeeding, of reaching the top, of learning new moves, of trying more difficult routes and being better than others. The combination of these extremes makes this sport so attractive to many people.

As shown in the following figure[1], climbing requires technical, physical and mental strength equally. That is one of the keys why this sport is so attractive to many people. Nevertheless most climbers fail to advance in at least one of these fields. Therefore "Climb Beyond" will help user to learn technical issues faster and feel mentally more secure.

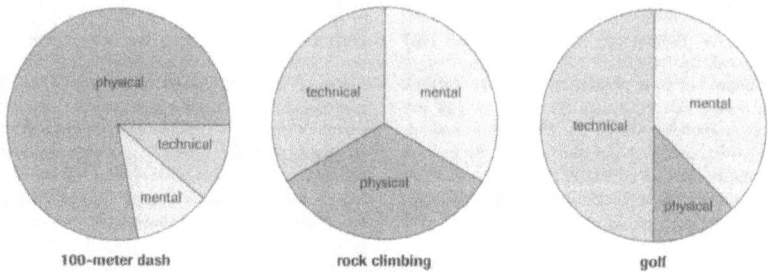

physical

technical

mental

technical   mental

physical

mental

technical

physical

100-meter dash   rock climbing   golf

The climbing market itself is divided into indoor and outdoor while indoor is the most attractive part for urbanized people. Furthermore the indoor market is divided into bouldering and rope climbing. "To boulder" means climbing on walls of smaller height without being secured and without any further technical equipment. "Rope climbing" allows people to climb up to a typical height of 8 to 24 meters being secured by a thin line that is held by a second person standing on the bottom. This requires specific knowledge about securing, using ropes and knots and using further optional technical security equipment. Even though rope climbing is more complicated, it is the more attractive part because if contains all the fear and joy listed above.

Many climbing instruction courses focus on rope climbing and the security issues that come along with it. Courses and prices vary on the level of difficulty and how advanced the participants are. For

---

[1] [Hoerst03]; Figure 1.1; page 5

instructors it is a challenge to teach every single participant separately or to even show them their own capabilities.

The indoor climbing market exploded from the late 1980's to the beginning of the new millennium. Western countries like the US, UK and Germany entered a saturation phase. For the companies that operate indoor climbing facilities it gets more and more difficult to have something new exciting for the active climbers and during summer period it is even more difficult to even fill the facility with visitors [BMC03].

"Climb Beyond" addresses all these issues. It helps instructors to discuss with the participants. It allows less experienced climbers to feel more secure on the wall where they are usually lost and afraid of height whenever they do not know how to continue. And it enables operators of indoor climbing facilities making their service more attractive.

3. Description of specific characteristics

"Climb Beyond" combines state-of-the art technology to give users the real climbing experience. It helps people to enjoy climbing and facing their fear. It helps them to advance faster while saving money on instruction courses because they might not need the advanced courses

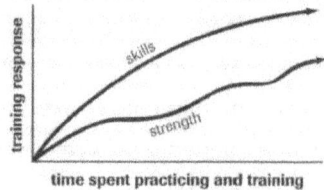

anymore. Without our service, anyone who starts climbing will experience kind of a logarithmic learning curve.[2] But for urbanized people a faster increase is of high interest. Therefore our service will increase the learning curve much faster in no time.

The service is easy to use, available all the time and does not cost tons of money. Extended services for accessing the tracked data allow anyone to review their own capabilities even at home. Because all the technology is put into a single small device, we can enhance any existing climbing facility by just installing the device and calibrating it to environmental conditions (point of view, light and shadow). There is no need to change anything else in the facility itself. Just the device and an Internet connection is required.

Body and movement tracking
Body recognition is a huge topic in the gaming industry. Devices like Nintendo® Wii™ and Sony® Eye-Toy™ allow players to use their body to interact freely with the game. But the real break-through was done

---

[2] [Hoerst03]; Figure 1.5; page 10

by Microsoft® with Kinect™ for XBox360™ because it really tracks one to 4 bodies (including skeleton data) at the same time and no additional technical equipment has to be held by the player. Kinect™ is the first device that has a computing power that is high enough and a latency low enough to give the player a smooth feeling of real interaction. Ten years ago this would have been like magic but nowadays every teenager knows about that topic and feels comfortable using this technology.

These technologies are of interest for indoor climbing because they allow detailed tracking of a human body. Within indoor climbing any device that does not need to be worn on the body has a clear advantage. Therefore only Microsoft® Kinect™ is of interest. But so far Microsoft® did not publish any commercial license and the device only works up to a distance of 3.5 meters. Typically distances in indoor climbing facilities are 3 to 10 meters. This is why a different method of using two cameras in a stereoscopic mode will be used. Tracking data includes:

- Video recording for later playback and teaching
- Distance information for terrain recognition and determining the distance of the climber between the camera device and to climbing wall
- Shape recognition of any human body for compressed data storage and laser re-projection

The advantages of these tracking methods are:

- re-usage of existing technology: Stereoscopic or cameras with depth/distance recognition are on the market
- re-usage of existing algorithms from the scientific field of computer graphics
- full body recognition: a complete human body is tracked and not only hands or feet
- no additional equipment:
  - people do not need to buy any new equipment
  - people do not need to wear anything on your body
  - no markers to put on hands (as used in motion capturing in film industry)

Body projection

The tracked data can easily be used for later review or teaching but the real advantage is the re-projection of the already tracked data of a professional climber onto the climbing wall to help any less experienced climber to advance and feel more secure. Projection can be done while climbing so that the next move from the current position is projected or to allow a step-by-step view to learn about the route while still standing on the ground.

The projection must be easy to see, bright enough and easy to understand. Indoor climbing walls are usually colored in white or light grey. Furthermore the environment is fully lightened by powerful lamps form opposite walls or ceiling. Therefore "Climb Beyond" introduces monochrome laser beam projection that everybody knows from laser show or laser pointer devices. The purposes are:

- mature and inexpensive technology
- security issues of laser beams are well known and easy to handle
- perfect contrast and brightness even under very bright environmental conditions
- low maintenance costs, low energy consumption and long life time
- compact design

A sample application how body tracking and shape projection might look like has been implemented within 5 hours using the freely available non-commercial version of Microsoft® Kinect™ Software Development Kit.[3] The sample shown in the upper left quad indicates how the black line following the shape of the body can be used for projection.

Depth Stream

Skeleton (rendered if full body fits in frame)

Color Video Stream

19 fps

[3] http://www.microsoft.com/en-us/Kinect™forwindows/download/

A sample graphic showing the different steps and shapes of climbing moves illustrates the recording and projection.

A sample graphic with the overlay of the different steps and shapes of climbing moves illustrates the purpose of recording and projection.

Usage and control

The device will be installed opposite of the climbing wall to get a good field of view so that a human body can be tracked easily and re-projection can be done without interfering others. There are only two modes to control - recording and projection. For both of them any user just needs to select a route that he or she wants to climb up. These routes are usually marked by handles of different colors and they are usually numbered or named by funny names. Therefore routes can easily be identified and chosen from a list or from an image of the wall showing all available routes. Controlling can be done by a simple remote control device or a touch panel. A touch panel allows easy selection of routes and displaying further information about difficulty or other special hints. Remote access from home or during teaching can be done by network connection or hosting a website or online community.

Network connection

Because the device is a complete package of body tracking and laser based re-projection, it can easily be installed. It comes with a embedded computer system including a network connection. This enables "Climb Beyond" to offer full featured services around indoor climbing. This includes:

- remote upgrade of service that are installed in the device
- remote maintenance
- remote access to recorded tracking data (for review and teaching)
- inter-connecting multiple facilities of the same operating company
- building an online community
- online teaching and learning
- optional cloud services to store and access data

4. Competition

Competition in the indoor climbing market

This application has wide spread competition. Any new service in the indoor climbing market is seen as direct competition. During the past 20 years indoor climbing facilities increased their size and numbers routes to attract more customers. But there is no high-tech equipment used. Most instruction courses are discussed directly during the lesson and while climbing. Sometimes mobile digital cameras are used to record a climber as a video clip and a regular video projection device is used for later discussion. This is also recording and re-projection but based on old technology without any interaction and it is not accessible to climbers when the instruction course has finished.

Technological competition

Other competition is seen in technology. There are companies that deal with cameras that allow depth recognition and there are companies dealing with laser projectors. But all of them are currently not active in the indoor climbing market. Camera manufacturers are only resellers mostly to the security and surveillance market. And laser technology is used in show effects or in high-end and expensive industrial or architectural applications.

Microsoft® Kinect™ for XBox360™ is the strongest competition in technology because it is very accurate in body and depth recognition and the reselling price (€ 140) is very low compared to the industry (€ 700 to € 10.000). Currently Microsoft® allows Kinect™ to be used in private or prototype applications but still there is no commercial licensing available. Furthermore the scanning distance ends at 3.5

meters which is too short for indoor applications. If Microsoft manages to increase this distance and offers a commercial license, Kinect™ might be used by "Climb Beyond".

5. Unique selling proposition

We combine existing well known mature technology to provide users with a new climbing experience. It is inexpensive to set up and easy to use by any climber or instructor. The laser re-projection gives any climber a unique experience how to move along the wall and to compare himself with the movements of any more advanced climber. Combining on-site real usage with remote data access allows users to feel more involved in indoor climbing sports and its community. For climbing facilities we provide a full service package on acceptable costs, providing remote maintenance, full upgrade service to new features and 24/7 remote support.

6. Assessment of opportunity

Private expenditures for leisure and fun

Indoor climbing is an activity that is done in people's free time. Therefore it belongs to the financial indicator of expenditures that are done for leisure and sports. Assessing the market data for climbing has to start on the overall expenditures of private households and public government in this sector. The publicly available data for this sector is given by the NACE codes for retail and wholesale as well as rental agencies for sports equipment. Unfortunately there are no NACE codes that go into the climbing sector in more detail. The following table is based on the data of the Federal Statistics Office of Germany.[4] Due to a change in methodology the data after 2009 is not comparable to the data before.

		2005	2009
Number of	Retail	2674	4609
Number of	Wholesale	550	1051
Employees	Retail	8103	14193
Employees	Wholesale	8103	14193
Business volume	Retail	2236 mill. €	3456 mill. €
Business volume	Wholesale	2660 mill. €	5096 mill. €

There is an obvious trend that the business for sports equipment is increasing. Most numbers nearly doubled within just five years. This fits another trend that people do have an increasing sensitivity for a healthy life style and that they are willing to spend more money for

---

[4] *"Data Report"*; 2005 to 2009; German Federal Statistics Office

it.[5] Some more reports and numbers are supporting this theory. The German Federal Statistics Office randomly publishes official surveys on specific research topics. Based on a report done on time usage for leisure and culture the following graphic is constructed.[6]

According to that data each single household spends on average 11% of the income on leisure and sports. This is 218 Euro a month which sums up to 2616 Euro annually.[7] In 2010 about 40 million households have been recorded [Census10]. Therefore the money spend on leisure activities sums up to 104 billion Euro annually. The same data reveals that 52% of the people in East Germany and 44% in the west are doing any sports at least once a week. The trend observed in the retail and wholesale industry for sports is the same in this data because the number of people doing sports on a regularly basis increased by more than 30% from 1998 to 2004. At the same time the number of people working in position that require higher qualifications increased from 33% in 1992 to 42% in 2010.[8] It can be assumed that these people do have a higher income that allows them to spend more money on leisure, sports and culture.

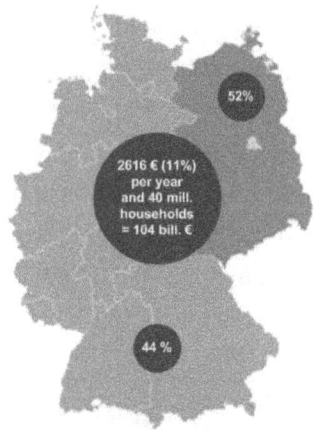

---

[5] [DATA_II_06]; chapter 10.2, page 530/531

[6] [DATA_II_06]; chapter 10.2, table 4, page 530

[7] [DATA_I_06]; chapter 6.2, page 149

[8] [Work10]; chapter 6.1, page 52

	1998	2004
East Germany	21	52
West Germany	31	44

Sports

Now that the data for leisure, sports and culture is known that data has to be split up to expenditures done on sports only and - if possible - on indoor climbing. There is not much recent data on climbing publicly available. Therefore the most current data for the United Kingdom and Germany is used evaluation and as a basic assumption for westernized countries.

In Germany 61% of the people that do sports at least once a week are summarized in a group that includes walking, jogging, hiking and climbing.[9] According to 81.2 million German citizens [Census10] there are around 36 million people[10] doing sports regularly and 22 million of them (61%) are doing one of the activities listed before. There is no official data that further divides this group of activities. But an invalidated assumption records 350.000 active climbers in Germany.[11] For the UK a number of 700.000 people in 1993 has been recorded which is an increase of 40% compared to 1989 and the subset of them who participate in indoor climbing amounts roughly to 74% [BMC03]. This number has been seen as still valid in 2003.

---

[9] [DATA_II_06]; chapter 10.2, figure 4, page 529

[10] assumption of 45% overall; because of 44% in West Germany and 52% in East Germany

[11] Mr Thomas Bucher; Public relations; German Alpine Association; Email dated Oct. 27th 2011

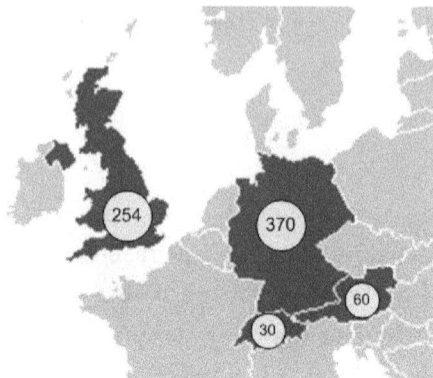

Based on these numbers 259.000 indoor climbers are assumed to be active in Germany. This defines a subset of 3 to 4% of the overall group of people that are active in walking, jogging, hiking or climbing. And about 60% of them are in an age between 18 to 39. This makes them an interesting target group.[12]

Another important report reveals that the public expenditures on recreation and sports increase from 1.1 billion Euros in 1970 to 5.7 billion Euro in 2003. From these 5.7 billion. Euro, 1.7 billion have been spent on the construction of sports facilities and another 1.1 billion on the promotion of sports.[13]

Indoor climbing facilities

So far only data about expenditures on leisure and sports has been analyzed. Another point of interest is the facilities where indoor climbing is done. These indoor climbing halls vary in geographic location, size, number of climbing routes and height. Valid data is available for the UK from 1998 to 2003 [BMC03] and for Germany in 2003 [GAA03].

---

[12] [DATA_II_06]; chapter 10.1, table 3, page 529
[13] [DATA_I_06]; chapter 6.2, page 149

According to that data there are about 370 climbing halls in Germany, 254 in the UK. Other unverified sources list another 60 halls in Austria, 30 in Switzerland, 600 halls in the US and 90 in Canada. The data also reveals the increasing trend of indoor climbing because the number of halls in the UK increased from 44 in 1988 to 254 in 1998 and in Germany from 250 in the middle of the 21st century to 370 in 2011.

The size and equipment of climbing facilities varies a lot. Therefore they are of different attractiveness to climbers. In Germany the most attractive and biggest halls are located in the south-west including Munich, Stuttgart and Cologne. But they are widely spread all over the country. The average calculated numbers[14] per facility in Germany are:

- 1.500 square meters in size
- 10 to 16 meter in height
- 100 to 400 different climbing routes

The German Alpine Association lists one facility in Munich as the largest climbing hall with a size of 8.000 square meters and second one in Duisburg with a size of 7.000 square meters. A third, also located in Munich, with a size of 3.750 square meters. In height they are listed with 34m in Munich, 31m in Leipzig and 18m in Dortmund. Of course these samples are exceptions but they underline the increasing interest in indoor climbing because most of facilities have been extended during the past 5 years due to increasing number of visitors. For example the largest in the area of Munich has been

---

[14] *"Background information: Climbing facilities in Germany"*; German Alpine Association; March 2003

extended from a size of 4.450 in 2009 to 8.000 square meters in 2011.[15]

Contacting the two largest climbing equipment manufacturers Back Diamond[16] and Mammut[17] did not lead to any new valid data. They redirected to the same sources of information that have been already used. This indicates that these sources are valid.

Capital concerns

The device, used for visual recording, tracking and re-projection, should be affordable for climbing facilities and the service offered by "Climb Beyond" must be priced at an acceptable level. The target price for the device is less than 5.000 Euro. Developing a prototype and installing it on a test site will not consume much money.

Because of the quite low target price, the cash flow for "Climb Beyond" highly depends on the pricing model and on the cooperation with operating companies that run climbing facilities. By selling the device itself no sustainable cash flow can be generated because the gross margin is low and the indoor climbing is a market of limited size. Once installed, no further cash flow is generated. Therefore a one-time payment is not an option. For the end user - the climber - there should be no or at least minimum additional costs to use our services on-site. Online services provided by "Climb Beyond" might be accessible at additional costs that have to be paid by the user itself.

---

[15] Mr Thomas Bucher; Public relations; German Alpine Association; Email dated Oct. 27th 2011

[16] http://www.blackdiamondequipment.com

[17] http://www.mammut.ch/

The device will be designed to observe about 5 to 10 different routes. Therefore an installation of 1 to 5 devices depending on the number of routes inside a facility is assumed. Because the device is limited to a good viewing angle onto routes, a total coverage of 10 to 40% per facility is assumed. Based on 259.000 active climbers the following calculation for the revenue of a facility can be done.

Entrance fee	10% coverage	40% coverage
	one visit	
6 Euro	155.400 Euro	621.600 Euro
10 Euro	259.000 Euro	1.036.000 Euro
12 Euro	310.800 Euro	1.243.200 Euro
	once a week (annually)	
6 Euro	8.080.800 Euro	32.323.200 Euro
10 Euro	13.468.000 Euro	53.872.000 Euro
12 Euro	16.161.600 Euro	64.646.400 Euro

These numbers reflect the revenue generated by all facilities in Germany. A licenses based pricing will be calculated on a desired share of these revenues.

Entrepreneurial self-assessment

I believe in the idea of "Climb beyond". All that is needed it is some time and the right team who also believes in it. There is nothing neither complicated nor non-realizable. The technology is already out there. It just needs to be assembled the right way. And the estimated time frame to do so is quite short. What thrills me is that the services around the central device can be extended step by step which gives the company time to grow and a future revenue stream. And once things are running well the idea of tracking and re-projecting can be used in various other industries in more attractive markets, too. But indoor climbing is a perfect point to start. I am a passionate climber myself and I went through all the stages of thrill and also disappointment. I know about the community and problems each single starter has to face.

Due to my German roots I am a more security oriented person. But my eyes have been opened up due to the study of economics and business in conjunction with the great lecturers that we had. And even though there are many ideas out there none of them could attract my attention as much as "Climb beyond" did.

What qualifies me to start this journey is my spirit and my determined character. People who know me from school, university, work and my current study know that I am a straight forward thinking and acting person. Someone who knows what to do to reach the goal and I am fast. And I am well aware that this can also been a negative side of a character. But knowing this should help me to balance to advantages and the disadvantages. From a professional point of view I have profound educations in both IT and business science and the past six years of work had a strong focus on computer graphics and vector based visualizations which are a key component within "Climb Beyond".

Entrepreneurial team

Due to my own study and current job the entrepreneurial team will be quite small until all data and the prototype have been verified to really start the business. Until then the highest focus will be on the research level. Making sure that the market need is valid and that the device will work. During this time we have to make sure that we align our strategy on time-to-business. The device itself and the first version of the software have to be assembled. The following list gives a short overview about the persons and their functions that are needed to setup the business.

- Matthias Heise: Most experiences business person summarizing technological and economic knowledge. I am responsible for financing, strategic alliances and public funding. During the research period I will make sure that we focus on our core competences.
- Jürgen Neuhuber: Skilled mountain guide and climbing instructor with a master in economics and business. He will build up the community around "Climb Beyond". Due to his extensive knowledge in climbing and his network to people in the community, he can make sure that our service is accepted.
- Chair of "Computer Graphics and Vision" at the Technical University of Graz: Due to widely available public funding for business-to-science co-operations, the chair will be a supporting factor on all technological issues for tracking peoples movements.
- Part-time team: In the first period of the company mostly part time employed students that result from the cooperation with the university, will be used for programming the software that is needed to run the device.

Once the business is running some more people have to be hired. First of all sales people to advertise our service in the German speaking region and second support people that can do on-site training, installation and remote-support.

7. Steps to a viable venture

To successfully setup "Climb Beyond" as a start-up with a sustainable future the following steps are required in sequential order.

1. In-depth market need analysis and user acceptance
2. Find cooperation and financing partner for prototype application
3. Prototype application to validate mathematical algorithms from computer graphics used for human body tracking and laser re-projection
4. Setup a research cooperation with a leading indoor climbing facility for on-site testing
5. Creating Business and Financial plan
6. Checking acceptance by presenting Business plan to operating companies of the 5 to 10 largest indoor climbing facilities in German speaking region
7. Presenting Business plan to commercial lending or other private investors
8. Getting detailed plans for device manufacturing
9. Finding hardware manufacture for contract based manufacturing of the device
10. Choosing start-up location for initial application and office location
11. Renting office and equipment
12. Designing and programming of software for the device
13. Installation of first 5 to 10 devices
14. Programming software services around the device
15. Attending related climbing and sports fairs in central Europe
16. Finding extended second round financing
17. Expansion into German speaking market

Step one will be done within my master-thesis in the end of the MBA study of "Entrepreneurship & Innovation". The second and third step will be done in cooperation with the Technical University of Graz and financed by the Austrian Association of the Promotion of Science.[18] Both institutions already accepted and approved the necessary steps. In the summer term in 2012 two or three students of computer science will work on a prototype. Step four will be done in the first quarter of 2012 to ensure that data for master-thesis and prototype can be validated by real climbers. Most likely the largest indoor climbing facility[19] in Graz will be a partner. This is a good decision because it is located close to my home and close to the Technical University of Graz. Furthermore the operating company runs several facilities all over Austria and might be interested in using the device.

Steps one to four are seen as a precondition for even setting up a venture. Its outcome will be the basis for any further decision and also for finding financing partners. These steps should be finished in autumn 2012. Steps 5 to 13 are the real setup of the company. This includes financing and building a stable secure business environment. If the prototype application shows good results these steps should be done within 3 month over the winter 2012 to 2013. They require my full attention and the support by computer science specialist for programming the software. It is planned that the students who worked on the prototype will continue to work for the start-up. Steps 13 to 17 will increase the revenue curve to allow to business to sustain and grow. The time horizon for these steps is the end of 2013 and the following two years. This also requires a larger team, one or

---

[18] "Österreichische Forschungsförderungsgesellschaft (FFG)"; http://www.ffg.at/

[19] City Adventure Center; http://www.c-a-c.at

two sales people and administrative personnel. My attention will shift to activities that ensure a sustainable business and finding long-term business partners.

8. Summary

"Climb Beyond" is a service that targets a very attractive consumer market. The entrepreneurial team will not be satisfied unless enthusiastic people have realized how this ease-of-use technology helps them to feel the fun and joy of indoor climbing. And no one can imagine in what other industries our service might be used in the future. The journey starts now!

9. Resources

Literature and other provides resources

- [Hoerst03] *"Training for Climbing"*; Eric J. Hörst; The Globe Pequot Press; 2003
- [Data_I_06] *"Leisure and Culture"*; chapter 6.2, page 149; Data Report 2006; Part I; German Federal Statistics Office
- [Data_II_06] *"Leisure activities & media usage"*; Data Report 2006, Part II; German Federal Statistics Office
- [Work10] *"Quality of work"*; chapter 6.1, page 52; German Federal Statistics Office; September 2010
- [Census10] *"Micro Census 2010"*; German Federal Statistics Office
- [BMC03] *"Participation Statistics"*; British Mountaineering Council; Updated version of 2003
- [GAA03] *"Background information: Climbing facilities in Germany"*; German Alpine Association; March 2003

Online resources

- http://www.mammut.ch
- http://www.blackdiamondequipment.com
- "Österreichische Forschungsförderungsgesellschaft (FFG)" http://www.ffg.at/

Contacts in person

- Mr Thomas Bucher; Public relations
  German Alpine Association; http://www.alpenverein.de
- Viola Wallrabenstein; Public Relations
  German Federal Statistics Office

- Bernhard Heßmann; Public Relations
  German Federal Statistics Office
- Mag. Stefan Kleinhappel
  City Adventure Center; http://www.c-a-c.at
- Dipl.-Ing. Hayko Riemenschneider
  Institute for Computer Graphics and Vision
  Technical University of Graz; http://www.icg.tugraz.at

NACE / Country codes for Germany

- Department of statistics in services and domestic trade;
  German Federal Statistics Office
- WZ08-461; Trading agencies
- WZ08-464; Wholesale of bicycles, sports and related equipment
- WZ08-476; Retail of sports and camping equipment (without
  camping furniture)
- WZ 77.21; Rental agencies for sport and other leisure
  equipment